Success With

Sight Words

SCHOLASTIC

Editor: Ourania Papacharalambous
Cover design by Tannaz Fassihi; cover illustration by Kevin Zimmer
Interior design by Cynthia Ng
Interior illustrations by Doug Jones

ISBN 978-1-338-79868-5
Scholastic Inc., 557 Broadway, New York, NY 10012
Copyright © 2022 Scholastic Inc.
All rights reserved. Printed in the U.S.A.
First printing, January 2022
1 2 3 4 5 6 7 8 9 10   40   29 28 27 26 25 24 23 22

INTRODUCTION

A relatively small number of words make up the great majority of text students will come across in the early elementary school years. If students can recognize these high-frequency words at a glance, they will have greater access to all the knowledge that awaits them. The best way to teach sight words is through practice and repetition. On page 4, you will find a list of the key skills covered in the activities throughout this book. *Scholastic Success With Sight Words* will help increase familiarity through games and activities designed to boost students' recognition of the top 100 sight words.

TABLE OF CONTENTS

Grade-Appropriate Skills Covered in *Scholastic Success With Sight Words*

Kindergarten

Follow words from left to right, top to bottom, and page by page.

Recognize that spoken words are represented in written language by specific sequences of letters.

Demonstrate command of the conventions of standard English grammar and usage when writing or speaking.

Print many upper- and lowercase letters.

Produce and expand complete sentences in shared language activities.

Write a letter or letters for most consonant and short-vowel sounds.

Spell simple words phonetically, drawing on knowledge of sound-letter relationships.

Grade 1

Recognize the distinguishing features of a sentence.

Demonstrate understanding of spoken words, syllables, and sounds.

Know and apply grade-level phonics and word analysis skills in decoding words.

Read with sufficient accuracy and fluency to support comprehension.

Demonstrate command of the conventions of standard English grammar and usage when writing or speaking.

Print all upper- and lowercase letters.

Demonstrate command of the conventions of standard English capitalization, punctuation, and spelling when writing.

Grade 2

Identify words with inconsistent but common spelling-sound correspondences.

Recognize and read grade-appropriate irregularly spelled words.

Read with sufficient accuracy and fluency to support comprehension.

Demonstrate command of the conventions of standard English grammar and usage when writing or speaking.

Demonstrate command of the conventions of standard English capitalization, punctuation, and spelling when writing.

What's Missing?

Fill in the boxes below to make words from the list.

① t

②  f

③ a  d

④

⑤  h e

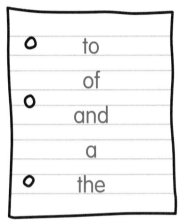

o   to
     of
o   and
     a
o   the

Use words from the list to complete the sentences.

① We ran out _____ milk.

② My dog is _____ beagle.

③ My friend _____ I like the same books.

④ I watered _____ plants today.

Scrambled Words

Unscramble the letters below to make words from the list.

1 uyo ___ ___ ___

2 si ___ ___

3 ttah ___ ___ ___ ___

4 ti ___ ___

5 ni ___ ___

in

is

you

that

it

Use words from the list to complete this card.

Thank _____ for the hat. _____

_____ just what I wanted! I hope _____

I will see you _____

the summer.

Copy & Circle

Read each word below. Copy it.
Then circle the word in the sentence.

Read.	Copy.	Circle.
1 in	_____	My bag was in the car.
2 is	_____	His coat is blue.
3 you	_____	You can come to my house.
4 that	_____	Take that book to school.
5 it	_____	I will eat it later.

Find and circle the words from the list in the story below.

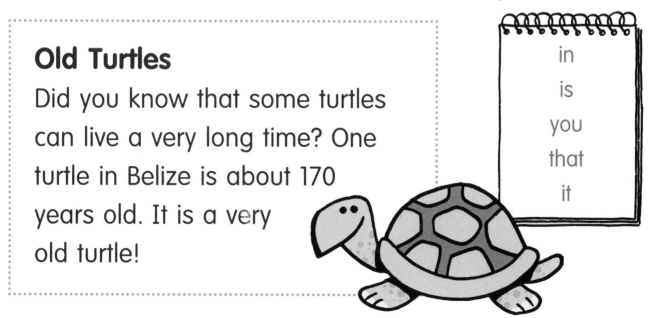

Old Turtles

Did you know that some turtles can live a very long time? One turtle in Belize is about 170 years old. It is a very old turtle!

in
is
you
that
it

What's Missing?

Fill in the boxes below to make words from the list.

1. w a ☐

2. f ☐ r

3. ☐ r e

4. h ☐

5. ☐ n

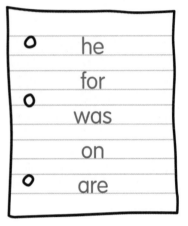

o	he
	for
o	was
	on
o	are

Use words from the list to complete the sentences.

1. Yesterday _____ my birthday.

2. You _____ my best friend.

3. I picked some flowers _____ my mom.

4. Tom put _____ his boots.

5. My dad said _____ would help me.

Code Words

Use this code to write sight words on the lines below.

| a ✖ | f ★ | n ▲ | r ● | w ◆ |
| e ♥ | h ➤ | o ✔ | s ■ | |

1 ★ ✔ ●

____ ____ ____

2 ✔ ▲

____ ____

3 ◆ ✖ ■

____ ____ ____

4 ➤ ♥

____ ____

5 ✖ ● ♥

____ ____ ____

Write each sight word once.

he _____   on _____

for _____   are _____

was _____

Scrambled Words

Unscramble the letters below to make words from the list.

1. hyet ___ ___ ___ ___

2. sa ___ ___

3. ta ___ ___

4. hsi ___ ___ ___

5. iwht ___ ___ ___ ___

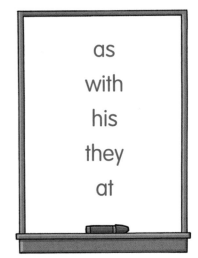

as
with
his
they
at

Use words from the list to complete this note.

Hey, Mom!

Dad is _____ Juan. _____ are

_____ the store. I saw Dad take _____

phone _____ he left. Give him a call.

Marco

Copy & Circle

Read each word below. Copy it.
Then circle the word in the sentence.

Read. **Copy.** **Circle.**

1 as _____ I'll be there as soon as I can.

2 with _____ Come with me to the movie.

3 his _____ Sam took his dog for a walk.

4 they _____ They are best friends.

5 at _____ I left my hat at school.

Find and circle four words from the list in the story below.

Pie-Eating Contest

Our town had a contest. Who could eat a pie the fastest? The pie eaters sat at a long table. They ate as fast as they could. My dad won! His pie was all gone in 5 minutes.

as
with
his
they
at

Hidden Picture

Find each space with be, this, from, I, and have.
Follow the directions below. What picture do you see?

If the word is **be**,
color the space

BROWN

If the word is **this**,
color the space

PINK

If the word is **from**,
color the space

YELLOW

If the word is **I**,
color the space

GREEN

If the word is **have**,
color the space

BLUE

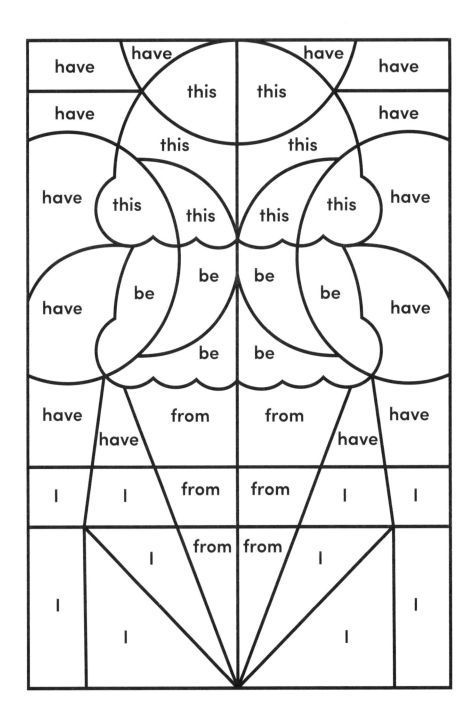

Copy & Circle

**Read each word below. Copy it.
Then circle the word in the sentence.**

Read.	**Copy.**	**Circle.**
1 be	_____	Pam will be at the mall.
2 this	_____	Is this your house?
3 from	_____	He walked home from school.
4 I	_____	Matt and I played catch.
5 have	_____	How many pets do you have?

Find and circle the words from the list in the note below.

A Note From Nana

To: Nick

From: Nana

I got this from my bookstore. If you
have it, tell me. It can be returned!

be

this

from

I

have

Code Words

Use this code to write sight words on the lines below.

| a ✖ | d ★ | h ▲ | o ● | t ◆ |
| b ❤ | e ➤ | n ✔ | r ■ | y ◗ |

1 ● ✔ ➤

____ ____ ____

4 ● ■

____ ____

2 ❤ ◗

____ ____

5 ▲ ✖ ★

____ ____ ____

3 ✔ ● ◆

____ ____ ____

Write each sight word once.

or _____

had _____

by _____

not _____

one _____

Word Search

Find the words in the puzzle below. Words are hidden ➔ and ↓.

be	from	have	one	this
by	had	not	or	

b	k	e	t	h	i	s	g	c	f
e	b	x	g	p	r	n	o	i	r
f	m	j	a	k	f	o	t	n	o
a	e	o	i	r	v	r	b	q	m
h	b	h	a	d	l	d	y	u	l
m	d	a	k	p	k	f	a	h	d
i	n	v	c	g	b	l	j	e	f
o	n	e	i	n	s	m	d	z	d
p	h	a	c	o	w	b	y	i	n
f	c	l	h	t	d	o	l	a	b

What's Missing?

Fill in the boxes below to make words from the list.

1. w h ☐ t

2. b ☐ t

3. ☐ h e n

4. w ☐ r e

5. ☐ l l

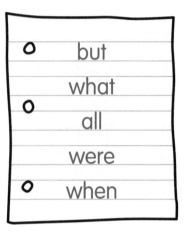

but
what
all
were
when

....

Use words from the list to complete the sentences.

1. She used _____ the eggs.

2. Tell me _____ the party is.

3. I want to go, _____ I am busy.

4. The ducks _____ wet.

5. _____ did you say?

Hidden Picture

Find each space with but, what, all, were, and when.
Follow the directions below. What picture do you see?

If the word is **but**,
color the space

RED

If the word is **what**,
color the space

PURPLE

If the word is **all**,
color the space

YELLOW

If the word is **were**,
color the space

GREEN

If the word is **when**,
color the space

BLUE

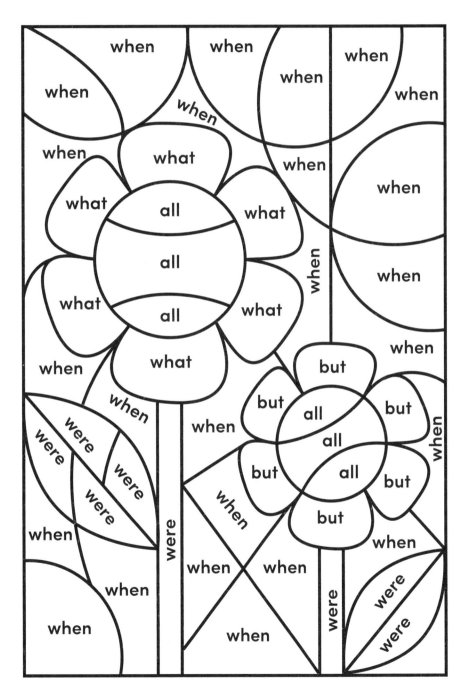

Scrambled Words

Unscramble the letters below to make words from the list.

1. anc ___ ___ ___

2. na ___ ___

3. ereth ___ ___ ___ ___ ___

4. yuro ___ ___ ___ ___

5. ew ___ ___

we
there
can
an
your

Find and circle the words from the list in the ad below.

Garage Sale!

Tons of stuff for sale.

Toys, clothes, books, dishes...even an oven!

We can meet all your needs.

Be there!

SALE

STUFFED TOYS

Code Words

Use this code to write sight words on the lines below.

a ✖   e ★   n ▲   r ●   u ◆   y ✚

c ♥   h ➤   o ✔   t ■   w ◗

1 ♥ ✖ ▲

_____ _____ _____

4 ✖ ▲

_____ _____

2 ◗ ★

_____ _____

5 ■ ➤ ★ ● ★

_____ _____ _____ _____ _____

3 ✚ ✔ ◆ ●

_____ _____ _____ _____

Write each sight word once.

we _____   an _____

there _____   your _____

can _____

Copy & Circle

Read each word below. Copy it.
Then circle the word in the sentence.

Read.   **Copy.**   **Circle.**

1 which _____ Which box do you want?

2 their _____ They took their time.

3 said _____ She said she was sorry.

4 if _____ We can stop if you get tired.

5 do _____ What do you want to eat?

Find and circle the words from the list in the note below.

Road Trip

This summer, I took a long car trip with my grandparents. They got two flat tires in one day! Their car was stuck on the road forever, which was not fun. My grandfather said if we do it again, we're taking the train!

which
their
said
if
do

Word Search

Find the words in the puzzle below. Words are hidden → and ↓.

can	if	their	we	your
do	said	there	which	an

e	h	q	k	x	c	s	u	o	b
n	a	y	a	w	h	i	c	h	w
i	d	o	m	g	b	d	a	u	h
r	e	u	v	p	u	o	a	n	l
s	n	r	e	y	c	t	p	r	c
t	l	e	g	s	a	i	d	r	x
h	r	b	v	i	n	t	r	f	a
e	j	i	f	j	d	i	n	c	w
i	g	p	s	h	t	h	e	r	e
r	w	d	o	y	n	z	m	y	t

Word Shapes

Write words from the list in the boxes below.
The boxes show you the shape of the letters.

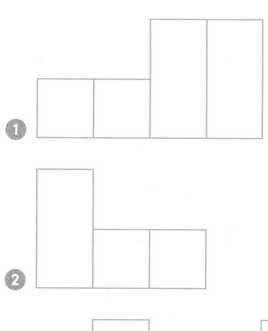

1

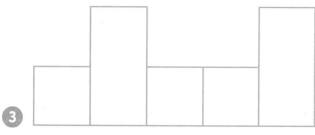

2

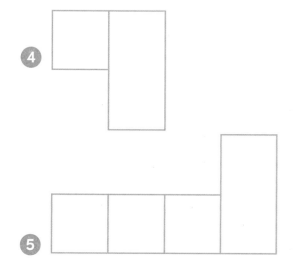

3

o	will
	each
o	about
	how
o	up

4

5

Hidden Picture

Find each space with will, each, about, how, **and** up.
Follow the directions below. What picture do you see?

If the word is **will**,
color the space

If the word is **each**,
color the space

If the word is **about**,
color the space

If the word is **how**,
color the space

If the word is **up**,
color the space

What's Missing?

Complete the sentences by using a letter from the magnifying glass to make a word from the list.

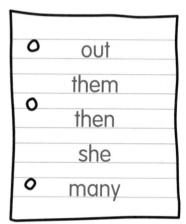

o   out

them

o   then

she

o   many

1. Can Henry come _____ut to play?

2. Eat first and the_____ we will go to town.

3. How man_____ pets do you have?

4. Please put th_____m away when you are done.

5. Does s_____e go to camp with you?

Going Places

Help the bird find its eggs. Connect a path by coloring each nest with a word from the list.

out
them
then
she
many

many   about

if   which   then   she

how   up   there   out

if   which   many   an

can   then   will   we

your   them   if   you

each   will   she

Word Shapes

Write words from the list in the boxes below.
The boxes show you the shape of the letters.

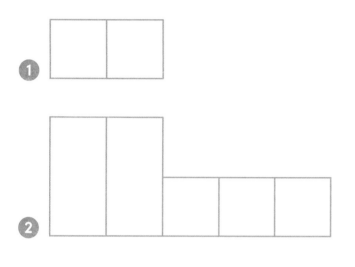

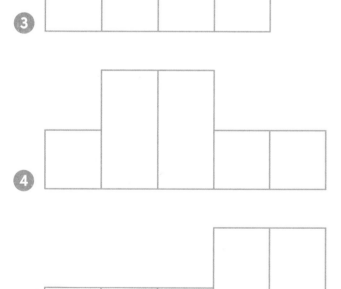

○	some
	so
○	these
	would
○	other

1

2

3

4

5

Scrambled Words

Unscramble the letters below to make words from the list.

1. eesht __ __ __ __ __

2. threo __ __ __ __ __

3. os __ __

4. mose __ __ __ __

5. wulod __ __ __ __ __

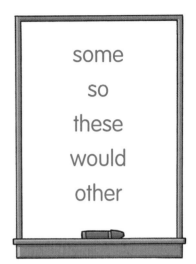

some

so

these

would

other

Use words from the list to complete these rhymes.

1. "Put _____ socks on," said his mother.

   "Here is one, and here's the _____.

2. "Spinach, carrots, broccoli, cheese,

   I won't have a bite of _____."

3. "You're _____ silly that you _____
   forget your head, if you could."

Code Words

Use this code to write sight words on the lines below.

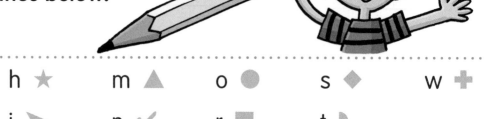

| a ✖ | h ★ | m ▲ | o ● | s ◆ | w ➕ |
| e 💚 | i ➤ | n ✔ | r ■ | t ◗ | |

1 ➤ ✔ ◗ ●

_____ _____ _____ _____

4 ★ 💚 ■

_____ _____ _____

2 ◗ ➕ ●

_____ _____ _____

5 ★ ✖ ◆

_____ _____ _____

3 ▲ ● ■ 💚

_____ _____ _____ _____

Draw a line to match the sight words.

into	has
has	more
more	two
her	into
two	her

Star Starters

Begin at the star. Follow the directions. Write the circled letters on the blanks to spell a word from the list.

Circle every third letter.

① g t m u m o d x r v q e

___ ___ ___ ___

⭐
② b t i m h n e k t s m o

___ ___ ___

Circle every fourth letter.

☆
③ m v e h u x s e p a z r

___ ___ ___

⭐
④ g r c h t y k a q p d s

___ ___ ___

⭐
⑤ j w i t o q u w m v y o

___ ___ ___

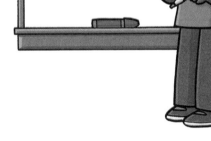

into
has
more
her
two

Scholastic Success With Sight Words **29**

Hidden Picture

Find each space with like, him, see, time, **and** could.
Follow the directions below. What picture do you see?

If the word is **like**,
color the space

GREEN

If the word is **him**,
color the space

RED

If the word is **see**,
color the space

YELLOW

If the word is **time**,
color the space

BLUE

If the word is **could**,
color the space

PINK

Word Search

Find the words in the puzzle below. Words are hidden → and ↓.

could	like	see	some	time
him	other	so	these	would

w	f	b	k	l	o	e	p	s	o
o	l	u	n	v	i	l	m	o	r
u	s	e	e	t	h	t	o	m	p
l	k	r	w	u	l	i	k	e	l
d	d	y	b	r	a	m	l	g	q
z	o	a	o	t	h	e	r	x	e
t	h	e	s	e	h	p	b	l	f
y	i	d	k	b	i	f	g	w	e
c	m	v	l	o	c	o	u	l	d
r	u	e	t	b	a	f	y	t	e

What's Missing?

Complete the sentences by using a letter from the magnifying glass to make a word from the list.

o no
make
o than
first
o been

1. I'm going to ma_____e dinner tonight.

2. She won fi_____st place in the race.

3. There are n_____ clouds in the sky.

4. Have you ever b_____en to the park?

5. I'd rather eat an apple th_____n a banana.

Copy & Circle

Read each word below. Copy it.
Then circle the word in the sentence.

Read.	**Copy.**	**Circle.**
1 no	_____	There are no bugs at the lake.
2 make	_____	Birds make nests in that tree.
3 than	_____	She'd rather play than work.
4 first	_____	She ran to first base.
5 been	_____	How have you been?

Find and circle the words from the list in the to-do list below.

My To-Do List!

1. First, make my bed
   (and Ben has to make his own).
2. Clean playroom (even though
   it's Ben's mess more than mine!).
3. Put away clothes that have
   been folded (by Ben!).
4. Be sure there are no weeds
   in garden. (Ben's job is to weed.)

no
make
than
first
been

TOY
BOX

Star Starters

Begin at the star. Follow the directions. Write the circled letters on the blanks to spell a word from the list.

Circle every other letter.

① i p u e t o r p m l w e

___ ___ ___ ___ ___ ___

Circle every fourth letter.

② b v a m p o g y k

___ ___ ___

Circle every third letter.

③ l z w y s h x m o

___ ___ ___

its

who

now

people

my

④ p w i a j t i c s

___ ___ ___ ___

⑤ m d n r e o s y w

___ ___ ___ ___

Scrambled Words

Unscramble the letters below to make words from the list.

1. sti ___ ___ ___

2. onw ___ ___ ___

3. ym ___ ___

4. woh ___ ___ ___

5. eelopp ___ ___ ___ ___ ___ ___

its
who
now
people
my

Use four words from the list to complete this email.

To: lizb@email.com
From: Gina
Subject: B'day Party

I can't wait for _____ birthday party. I still don't know
_____ is coming. There might be 22 _____!
As of _____, there will be 17 guests.
See you soon!
Gina

Hidden Picture

Find each space with made, over, did, down, and only.
Follow the directions below. What picture do you see?

If the word is **made**,
color the space

PURPLE

If the word is **over**,
color the space

PINK

If the word is **did**,
color the space

GREEN

If the word is **down**,
color the space

YELLOW

If the word is **only**,
color the space

BLUE

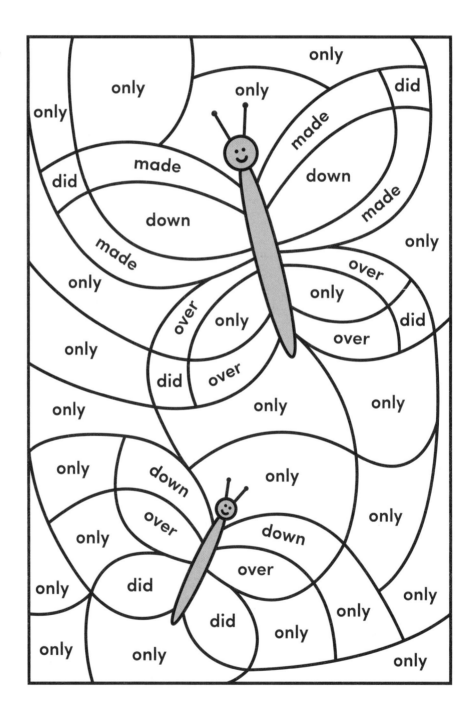

Going Places

Help the girl reach the basket by coloring each ball that has a word from the list.

made
over
did
down
only

can

over

made

only

he

did

down

did

like

made

then

how

only

START

Word Shapes

Write words from the list in the boxes below.
The boxes show you the shape of the letters.

1

2

3

4

5

○	way
○	find
○	use
	may
○	water

Code Words

Use this code to write sight words on the lines below.

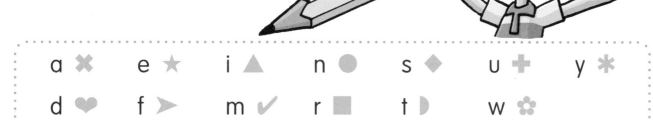

a ✖   e ★   i ▲   n ●   s ◆   u ✚   y ✳
d ❤   f ➤   m ✔   r ■   t ◗   w ✿

1

___ ___ ___

2 ✚ ◆ ★

___ ___ ___

3 ✔ ✖ ✳

___ ___ ___

4

___ ___ ___ ___ ___

5 ➤ ▲ ● ❤

___ ___ ___ ___

Draw a line to match the sight words.

way	find
find	use
use	may
may	water
water	way

Scholastic Success With Sight Words   **39**

Connect It!

Connect the letters in the first column with letters in the second to make words from the list. Then write the word next to the numbers below.

1. lo   ter

2. wo   tle

3. lit   ng

4. af   ry

5. ve   rds

long
little
very
after
words

1. _____

2. _____

3. _____

4. _____

5. _____

Scrambled Words

Unscramble the letters below to make words from the list.

1. lttile __ __ __ __ __ __

2. wrdos __ __ __ __ __

3. ratef __ __ __ __ __

4. evyr __ __ __ __

5. lgon __ __ __ __

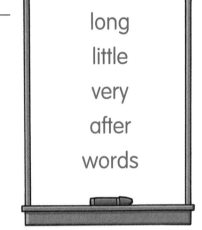

long
little
very
after
words

Use words from the list to complete the note.

Dear Maria,

This is just a _____ note to thank you for

helping at the bake sale. You were there for a _____

_____ time! _____ the sale, we

had enough money for our class trip. There are no

_____ to thank you enough!

Star Starters

Begin at the star. Follow the directions. Write the circled letters on the blanks to spell a word from the list.

Circle every other letter.

⭐
1 b c p a m l f l x e w d

___ ___ ___ ___ ___ ___

⭐
2 g w l h o e a r t e

___ ___ ___ ___ ___

Circle every third letter.

⭐
3 m h k f z n p y o e s w

___ ___ ___ ___

⭐
4 v c m c z o l t s j i t

___ ___ ___ ___

⭐
5 l c j r w u x m s p o t

___ ___ ___ ___

called
just
where
most
know

Hidden Picture

Find each space with called, just, where, most, and know.
Follow the directions below. What picture do you see?

If the word is **called**,
color the space

If the word is **just**,
color the space

ORANGE

If the word is **where**,
color the space

BLUE

If the word is **most**,
color the space

RED

If the word is **know**,
color the space

GREEN

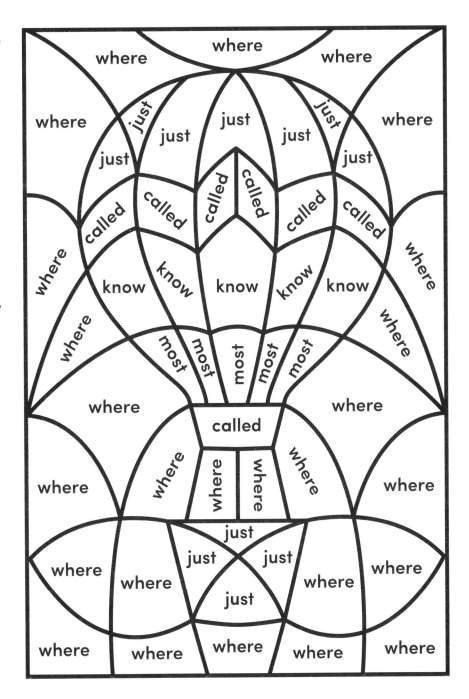

Word Search

Find the words in the puzzle below. Words are hidden → and ↓.

about	each	her	many	than	was	with
and	from	his	not	that	were	you
are	have	long	one	the	what	

r	s	t	m	v	o	e	l	y	w	a	s	w
h	a	r	e	i	t	h	l	b	e	p	r	h
o	t	s	a	z	p	f	w	n	r	u	c	g
h	j	d	c	s	r	r	a	k	e	n	l	s
w	v	b	h	a	b	o	u	t	k	t	h	t
h	e	r	e	n	c	m	c	g	y	o	b	h
a	a	l	n	d	n	t	e	l	o	n	g	a
t	g	p	m	n	e	h	a	o	u	h	t	t
h	c	x	h	e	r	a	l	u	b	d	h	t
m	i	u	g	d	k	n	s	v	x	q	e	w
o	n	e	o	n	t	r	u	h	a	v	e	i
y	o	o	r	e	f	m	t	i	e	j	e	t
a	t	w	m	a	n	y	h	s	t	r	v	h

Word Search

Find the words in the puzzle below. Words are hidden ➜ and ↓.

been	find	know	make	now	people	water
called	into	little	more	out	them	words
down	just	made	most	over	very	

a	c	l	f	i	n	d	q	h	p	r	m
j	t	i	m	x	l	j	u	s	t	w	o
n	h	n	k	a	o	c	h	m	i	o	s
c	e	t	h	c	f	a	e	a	b	r	t
e	m	o	r	e	m	l	z	k	e	d	d
l	i	d	b	a	h	l	o	e	u	s	e
i	p	e	o	p	l	e	j	m	a	d	e
t	g	t	v	x	l	d	q	u	n	a	n
t	b	e	e	n	k	n	o	w	o	u	t
l	n	r	r	p	d	e	z	c	w	r	v
e	i	l	s	w	a	t	e	r	o	i	f
o	v	e	r	y	m	s	n	d	o	w	n

100 Words List

a	find	know	out	two
about	first	like	over	up
after	for	little	people	use
all	from	long	said	very
an	had	made	see	was
and	has	make	she	water
are	have	many	so	way
as	he	may	some	we
at	her	more	than	were
be	him	most	that	what
been	his	my	the	when
but	how	no	their	where
by	I	not	them	which
called	if	now	then	who
can	in	of	there	will
could	into	on	these	with
did	is	one	they	words
do	it	only	this	would
down	its	or	time	you
each	just	other	to	your

ANSWER KEY

Page 5
1. to **2.** of **3.** and **4.** a **5.** the
1. of **2.** a **3.** and **4.** the

Page 6
1. you **2.** is **3.** that **4.** it **5.** in
Thank <u>you</u> for the hat. <u>It is</u> just what I wanted. I hope <u>that</u> I will see you <u>in</u> the summer.

Page 7
Did (you) know (that) some turtles can live a very long time? One turtle (in) Belize (is) about 170 years old. (It) is a very old turtle!

Page 8
1. was **2.** for **3.** are **4.** he **5.** on
1. was **2.** are **3.** for **4.** on **5.** he

Page 9
1. for **2.** on **3.** was **4.** he **5.** are

Page 10
1. they **2.** as **3.** at **4.** his **5.** with
Hey, Mom! Dad is <u>with</u> Juan. <u>They</u> are <u>at</u> the store. I saw Dad take <u>his</u> phone <u>as</u> he left. Give him a call. Marco

Page 11
Our town had a contest. Who could eat a pie the fastest? The pie eaters sat (at) a long table. They ate (as) fast (as) (they) could. My dad won! (His) pie was all gone in 5 minutes.

Page 13
To: Nick (From): Nana
(I) got (this) (from) my bookstore. If you (have) it, tell me. It can (be) returned!

Page 14
1. one **2.** by **3.** not **4.** or **5.** had

Page 15
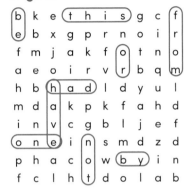

Page 16
1. what **2.** but **3.** when
4. were **5.** all
1. all **2.** when **3.** but
4. were **5.** What

Page 18
1. can **2.** an **3.** there
4. your **5.** we
Tons of stuff for sale. Toys, clothes, books, dishes... even (an) oven! (We) (can) meet all (your) needs. Be (there)!

Page 19
1. can **2.** we **3.** your
4. an **5.** there

Page 20
This summer, I took a long car trip with my grandparents. They got two flat tires in one day! (Their) car was stuck on the road forever, (which) was not fun. My grandfather (said) (if) we (do) it again, we're taking the train!

Page 21

Page 22
1. will **2.** how **3.** about
4. up **5.** each

Page 24
1. out **2.** then **3.** many
4. them **5.** she

Page 26
1. so **2.** these **3.** some
4. other **5.** would

Page 27
1. these **2.** other **3.** so
4. some **5.** would
1. some, other **2.** these
3. so, would

Page 28
1. into **2.** two **3.** more
4. her **5.** has

Page 29
1. more **2.** into **3.** her
4. has **5.** two

Page 31

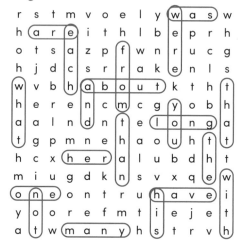

w f b k l o e p s o
o l u n v i l m o r
u s e e t h t o m p
l k r w u l i k e l
d d y b r a m l g q
z o a o t h e r x e
t h e s e h p b l f
y i d k b i f g w e
c m v l o c o u l d
r u e t b a f y t e

Page 32

1. make 2. first 3. no
4. been 5. than

Page 33

1. First , make my bed
(and Ben has to make his own).
2. Clean playroom (even though
it's Ben's mess more than mine!).
3. Put away clothes that have
been folded (by Ben!).
4. Be sure there are no weeds
in garden. (Ben's job is to weed.)

Page 34

1. people 2. my 3. who
4. its 5. now

Page 35

1. its 2. now 3. my
4. who 5. people
I can't wait for my birthday party.
I still don't know who is coming.
There might be 22 people! As of
now, there will be 17 guests.

Page 38

1. find 2. way 3. use
4. may 5. water
Note: way and may are
transposable.

Page 39

1. way 2. use 3. may
4. water 5. find

Page 40

1. long 2. words 3. little
4. after 5. very

Page 41

1. little 2. words 3. after
4. very 5. long
This is just a little note to thank
you for helping at the bake sale.
You were there for a very long
time! After the sale, we had
enough money for our class trip.
There are no words to thank you
enough!

Page 42

1. called 2. where
3. know 4. most 5. just

Page 44

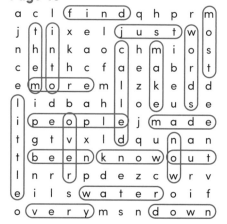

r s t m v o e l y w a s w
h a r e i t h l b e p r h
o t s a z p f w n r u c g
h j d c s r r a k e n l s
w v b h a b o u t k t h t
h e r e n c m c g y o b h
a a l n d n t e l o n g a
t g p m n e h a o u h t t
h c x h e r a l u b d h t
m i u g d k n s v x q e w
o n e o n t r u h a v e i
y o o r e f m t i e j e t
a t w m a n y h s t r v h

Page 45

a c l f i n d q h p r m
j t i x e l j u s t w o
n h n k a o c h m i o s
c e t h c f a e a b r t
e m o r e m l z k e d d
l i d b a h l o e u s e
i p e o p l e j m a d e
t g t v x l d q u n a n
t b e e n k n o w o u t
l n r r p d e z c w r v
e i l s w a t e r o i f
o v e r y m s n d o w n

48   Scholastic Success With Sight Words

© Scholastic Inc.